ICONS

TIMOTHÉE CHALAMET

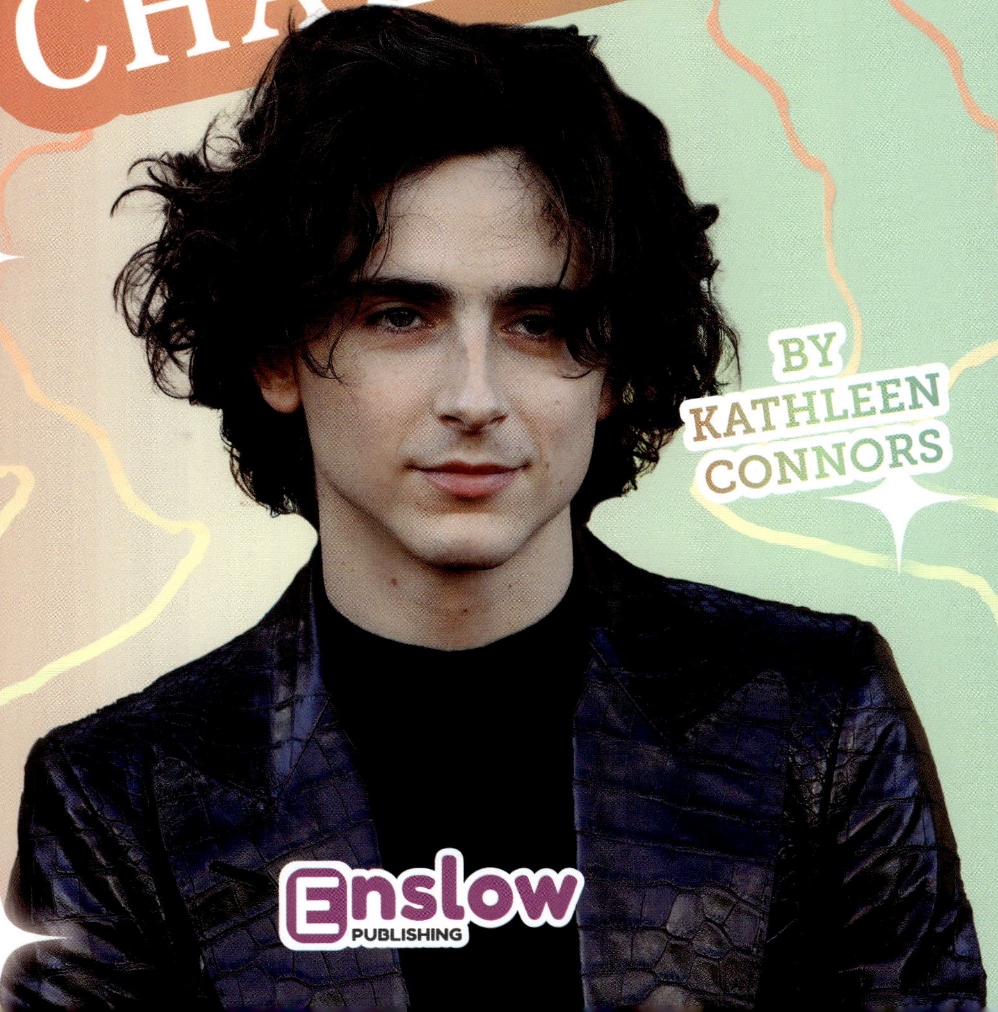

BY KATHLEEN CONNORS

Enslow PUBLISHING

Please visit our website, www.enslow.com.
For a free color catalog of all our high-quality books, call toll free 1-800-398-2504 or fax 1-877-980-4454.

Cataloging-in-Publication Data
Names: Connors, Katheleen.
Title: Timothée Chalamet / Katheleen Connors.
Description: Buffalo, NY : Enslow Publishing, 2026. | Series: Icons | Includes glossary and index.
Identifiers: ISBN 9781978544604 (pbk.) | ISBN 9781978544611 (library bound) | ISBN 9781978544628 (ebook)
Subjects: LCSH: Chalamet, Timothée--Juvenile literature. | Motion picture actors and actresses--Biography--Juvenile literature. | Actors--Biography--Juvenile literature.
Classification: LCC PN2287.C467 C66 2026 | DDC 791.4302'8092--dc23

Published in 2026 by
Enslow Publishing
2544 Clinton Street
Buffalo, NY 14224

Designer: Tanya Dellaccio Keeney
Editor: Kristen Rajczak Nelson

Photo credits: Cover Kathy Hutchins/Shutterstock.com; p. 5 NurPhoto SRL/Alamy Images; p. 7 Abaca Press/Alamy Images; pp. 9, 16 Album/Alamy Images; p. 10 WENN Rights Ltd/Alamy Images; pp. 11, 15 Photo 12/Alamy Images; p. 13 UPI/Alamy Images; p. 17 PA Images/Alamy Images; p. 19 dpa picture alliance/Alamy Images; p. 21 BFA/Alamy Images; p. 22 Entertainment Pictures/Alamy Images; p. 23 FlixPix/Alamy Images; p. 24 Barry King/Alamy Images; p. 25 Geisler-Fotopress GmbH/Alamy Images; p. 27 Image Press Agency/Alamy Images; p. 29 Sipa/Alamy Images.

Printed in the United States of America

CPSIA compliance information: Batch #CSENS26: For further information contact Enslow Publishing, at 1-800-398-2504.

Contents

ICONIC TALENT 4
FAMILY TIES 6
YOUNG PERFORMER 8
THE BIG ONE? 10
TIMMY'S BIG YEAR 12
LOVING LAURIE 16
FASHION ICON 18
HEADING TO ARRAKIS 20
MUSIC MAN 22
BECOMING BOB 24
TIM AT THE TOP 28
TIMELINE 30
FOR MORE INFORMATION 31
GLOSSARY 32
INDEX 32

Words in the glossary appear in **bold** the first time they are used in the text.

Iconic Talent

There's no question about it: Timothée Chalamet is an **icon**! He made a name for himself in smaller movies and now stars in big blockbusters. His **career** started when he was just a teenager—and he's still working hard to be a top actor!

ICONIC!

*Before he turned 30, Timothée had already worked with some of the biggest **directors** in the world, including Wes Anderson, Greta Gerwig, and Christopher Nolan.*

29, SOLO

Family Ties

Timothée was born on December 27, 1995, in New York City. His mom was a dancer on Broadway and an actress. His father was born in France and worked for **UNICEF**. Timothée has a sister named Pauline.

ICONIC!

Timothée comes from a family of ***performers****. His grandmother was also a dancer on Broadway, and his sister dances ballet!*

Young Performer

Timothée has been performing since he was a kid. He went to a special high school for the performing arts. As a teenager, he started getting small parts on TV shows, including *Royal Pains* and *Homeland*. He also appeared in plays.

ICONIC!

While growing up, Timothée spent his summers near the city of Lyon, France.

Timothée in Royal Pains

The Big One?

Timothée finished high school in 2013. The following year, he appeared in a hit movie called *Interstellar*. Timothée hoped it would be his big break—but the part was smaller than he thought it would be. He decided to go to college.

Timothée in Interstellar

ICONIC!

Timothée took classes at Columbia University and New York University.

Timmy's Big Year

Timothée found that he just wanted to be an actor and left college. He also started getting more movie offers. In 2017, Timothée starred in several movies, including *Lady Bird* and *Hostiles*, that put him in the spotlight.

ICONIC!

Timothée said that working with the director of Lady Bird, *Greta Gerwig, and the other actors in the movie helped him decide to "**dedicate**" himself to acting.*

Call Me by Your Name also came out in 2017. Moviegoers and **critics** alike recognized Timothée's talent. At age 22, he became the youngest actor to be **nominated** for best actor at the Academy Awards in 80 years!

ICONIC!

Timothée speaks French as well as English. He learned to speak Italian as well when making Call Me by Your Name!

Timothée in Call Me by Your Name

Loving Laurie

In 2019, Timothée appeared in another Greta Gerwig movie. He played Laurie in *Little Women*. It was nominated for best picture (movie) at the Academy Awards! Timothée was proud of his success—but he still had more he wanted to do.

Timothée as Laurie

ICONIC!

Timothée was told he wasn't right for parts in action movies he tried out for, including The Maze Runner, *because of his tall, thin build.*

Fashion Icon

By this time, Timothée was well-known. He was often on the red carpet at awards shows. Timothée made bold fashion choices. He was also starting to be featured in ads for high-end brands like Chanel and Cartier.

ICONIC!

Timothée doesn't have a stylist, or a person who chooses what he will wear. He picks it all out himself!

Heading to Arrakis

In 2021, Timothée became even more iconic! He starred as Paul Atreides in *Dune: Part One*. It was Timothée's biggest movie yet, and his first role, or part, in a movie that had a lot of action. He gave a great performance!

ICONIC!

Dune: Part Two came out in 2024. Timothée starred with other iconic young actors, including Zendaya, Austin Butler, and Florence Pugh.

Music Man

Timothée showed yet another side of his talent in 2023. He played Willy Wonka in the musical movie *Wonka*. He trained hard to get the dancing just right. In fact, he learned how to tap dance for the role!

Timothée as Willy Wonka

ICONIC!

Timothée didn't star in musicals in high school. He says he lost parts to schoolmate—and now fellow actor—Ansel Elgort!

Becoming Bob

In 2024, Timothée starred in *A Complete Unknown*. He played music icon Bob Dylan. In fact, Timothée had been preparing to play the role for years. He took guitar, singing, and harmonica lessons. He also learned how to talk like Dylan.

Timothée as Bob Dylan

ICONIC!

At first, Timothée only had a few months to get ready to play Dylan. The COVID-19 ***pandemic*** *was part of what slowed the making of the movie.*

Timothée gave his all to making *A Complete Unknown*. The work paid off: He was nominated for best actor at the Academy Awards again! The movie was also nominated for best picture.

ICONIC!

Timothée told Rolling Stone*: "I had three months of my life to play Bob Dylan, after five years of preparing to play him. So while I was in it, that was my* **eternal** *focus. [Dylan] deserved that and then more."*

A COMPLETE UNKNOWN
A COMPLETE UNKNOWN
A COMPLETE UNKNOWN

Tim at the Top

Timothée rose to fame quickly and at a young age. His talent and hard work have kept him on top ever since—and he's not done yet. What will this icon accomplish next?

ICONIC!

Timothée produces movies as well as stars in them! This means he is part of every step of making a movie.

Timeline

1995	Timothée is born in New York City.
2013	He finishes high school.
2014	He appears in Interstellar.
2017	He appears in Call Me by Your Name and Lady Bird.
2018	He is nominated for best actor at the Academy Awards.
2019	He stars in Little Women.
2021	He stars in Dune: Part One.
2023	He stars in Wonka.
2024	He stars in Dune: Part Two and A Complete Unknown.
2025	He is nominated for best actor at the Academy Awards.

For More Information

BOOKS

Allen, Nafeesh. *What You Never Knew About Timothée Chalamet*. North Mankato, MN: Capstone Press, 2024.

Andrews, Elizabeth. *Timothée Chalamet: Dune's Leading Man*. Minneapolis, MN: DiscoverRoo, an imprint of Pop!, 2024.

WEBSITE

Timothée Chalamet

https://www.imdb.com/name/nm3154303/

Follow what Timothée does next.

Instagram: Timothée Chalamet

https://www.instagram.com/tchalamet/#

Keep up with Timothée here.

Publisher's note to educators and parents: Our editors have carefully reviewed these websites to ensure that they are suitable for students. Many websites change frequently, however, and we cannot guarantee that a site's future contents will continue to meet our high standards of quality and educational value. Be advised that students should be closely supervised whenever they access the internet.

Glossary

career: The job someone chooses to do for a long time.

critic: Someone whose job it is to talk or write about what they think of the arts, such as movies or books.

dedicate: Commit.

director: Someone in charge of the filming of a movie.

eternal: Main.

icon: A person who is very successful and admired.

nominate: To suggest someone for an honor.

pandemic: A time when a disease, or sickness, spreads quickly and affects a large number of people in a place or throughout the world.

performer: One who performs, or plays music, sings, or dances.

UNICEF: Part of the United Nations that works to make life better for children around the world.

Index

Academy Awards, 14, 16, 26, 30
A Complete Unknown, 24, 26, 30
Call Me by Your Name, 14, 30
Dune movies, 20, 21, 30
family, 6, 7
France, 6, 8
Gerwig, Greta, 4, 13, 16
Interstellar, 10, 30
Lady Bird, 12, 13, 30
Little Women, 16, 30
school, 8, 10, 11, 12, 30
Wonka, 22, 30

ICONS

TITLES IN THIS SERIES

ARIANA GRANDE

DWAYNE JOHNSON

PEDRO PASCAL

SABRINA CARPENTER

TIMOTHÉE CHALAMET

ZENDAYA

ISBN: 9781978544604

9 781978 544604

Enslow PUBLISHING

ICONS

PEDRO PASCAL

KATHLEEN CONNORS